Two generations ago I promised my first grandson I would write him a book. So now I dedicate my first published children's book to Justin .... and his children.

... never too late to pursue a dream.

— Nina Adams

Nina Adams
Loveland, Colorado

Printed in the United States of America

Silly Sally Squirrel
and the Sneaky Cat

Written by Nina Adams   Illustrated by Shaundra Schultz

"Mother, Mother, wake up! Please! May we go now?" Sally cried, as she bounced on Sammy to be sure he was awake too.

"Calm down, Sally," groaned her brother, scooting out of her way.

Last night Mother had promised she would show them where she found the nuts she sometimes brought them.

The sun was just peeping up, turning the sky pink and red.
Mother stretched and smiled.
"All right, let's go find our breakfast."
Half way down the big tree, Mother stopped and looked all around.
"It is best to know the whereabouts of Dog and Cat," she warned.
"Dog always barks when he sees us, but Cat moves very quietly.
You must watch carefully for him."

It was scary to jump right up to the windowsill of the house like Mother.

"You can always check here," Mother was saying, "Sometimes there is fruit, nuts, or something dark and sweet; a nice change from the seeds we find in the field."

But Sally was impatient.

"What's over here?" she asked as she hopped from the windowsill and ran around the corner of the house.

"Wait for us!" cried Mother.

But Sally was already out of sight when Mother and Sammy rounded the corner.

They bounded on across the big yard and soon saw Sally coming out of some bushy plants. She looked very pleased with herself. Mother was not pleased.

"Back to our home tree," she ordered. "Sally, you must learn to obey the rules!"

The rest of the day, Sally and Sammy played tag all over their big tree. Sally said nothing about the bushy plants. She was secretly planning to go back there very early in the morning.

In under the waving leaves she had found some delicious red berries.

The sun had not yet turned the sky bright when Sally woke.
She eased down the tree ever so quietly and ran to the plants.

She ate all the red berries and even some that were only partly red, until she could hold no more.

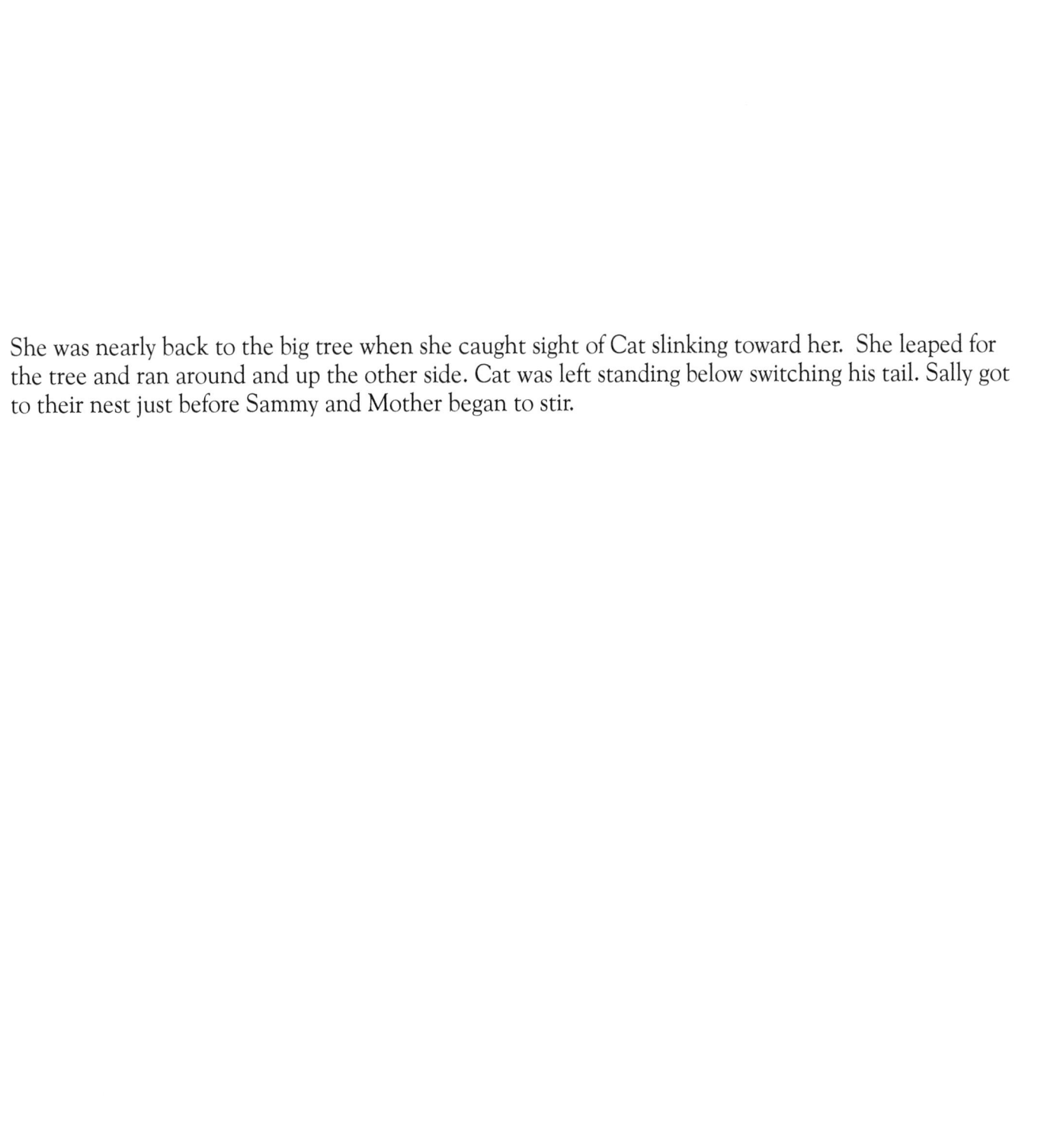

She was nearly back to the big tree when she caught sight of Cat slinking toward her. She leaped for the tree and ran around and up the other side. Cat was left standing below switching his tail. Sally got to their nest just before Sammy and Mother began to stir.

When the three of them started out for their breakfast that morning, Sally was not nearly so excited. In fact, Sally's tummy was not feeling very well.

Sammy liked playing in their big tree with Sally, but that afternoon she just wanted to lie on a limb and nap. Sammy was puzzled.

By next morning Sally was feeling much better. The thought of those delicious berries sent her out early again. This time her movements disturbed her brother. It took Sammy a few minutes to realize that Sally had left their tree. He decided he had better follow her. Sammy sometimes worried about his silly, sassy sister.

Sammy started across the yard. He saw Sally's tail disappear into the bushy plants. He also saw something else. Cat was sneaking toward Sally.

"Run! Run, Sally!" cried Sammy.
Without thinking, he rushed at Cat and then
turned and dashed up the little tree close by.
This seemed to confuse Cat for a moment and
Sally had time to run up the tree too.

Sally and Sammy jumped over to the roof of the house where they felt safer. When they had caught their breath, Sally said, "Thank you, Sammy. If you had not come, Cat might have gotten me."

"Why did you sneak out alone?" asked Sammy.

Sally hung her head.

"I was trying to keep the delicious red berries I found all to myself."

By this time Mother had come across the roof and heard Sally's confession.

"Oh! Sally, what a silly little squirrel you are. I should be very cross, but perhaps your fright will last longer than my scolding."

"Would you like to try the berries now?" asked Sally.

"Yes," said Mother. "I think a family breakfast together is a much better idea. Cat seems to be gone for now, but I think you had better keep him in mind."

I surely will! thought Sally. *I have a plan for Cat.*

That afternoon Sally and Sammy were playing in their tree.
"I'm going to see if I can see Cat from here." Sally said.
"You better be careful!" warned her brother.
Sally ran out on a limb and looked all around.
"Where are you Cat? Here Cat, Cat." She chattered.

"COME
AND GET ME,
CAT."

Cat came running. This time he leaped for the tree trunk and started climbing.

"Can't catch me!" taunted Sally as she climbed higher up the tree. Around and up Sally led Cat, chattering at him all the way. The limbs were getting smaller. Finally Sally ran out on one of the limbs and turned to look back at Cat as if she could go no farther. Cat followed. Sally backed up. Cat advanced toward Sally.

The limb was bending with their weight.
"Can't get me, Cat!" said Sally. "Can't climb, can't get me!"

With that, Sally leapt lightly to the branch above. The limb she left sprang up and down, catching Cat completely by surprise.

He lost his balance and his grip on the limb and tumbled toward the ground, snatching and grabbing at limbs on the way.

Of course he lit on his feet, as cats always do.

Sally, Sammy and Mother Squirrel laughed and laughed as they watched Cat march off across the yard, shaking each stinging paw with every step. When Sammy could catch his breath, he said, "Sally, that was a wonderful idea! Maybe you are not such a silly squirrel after all."